Creatures of the Night

edited by
Roger Caras

foreword by
Roger Tory Peterson

Westover
Publishing Company

A Media General Publication, Richmond, Virginia

DEDICATION . . . . .

For Gene, a friend . . . . .

Prepared in cooperation with
Photo Researchers, Inc.,
New York, New York.

Printed in U.S.A.
ISBN 0-87858-051-4

INTRODUCTION

The world at night is as foreign to most people as the surface of another planet. Even the most ardent naturalist can barely penetrate the secrets of the darkest hours. We are visually oriented and we don't see well at night—and that locks us out of some of nature's great adventures.

We are naturally envious, I think, of animals like the great wild cats that can cross back and forth between a diurnal and a nocturnal existence. I don't think we envy the timorous beasties that are held prisoner by the nocturnal pattern; it is those that can move in and out of it as easily as we pass through the shadow of a tree that make us envious.

If we are to understand anything of the night, we have to learn to listen much more carefully than we normally do. A blind person, of course, is better suited to the task than one who is sighted. Even then, though, even for a critical listener the night is a marvelously mysterious place.

Roger Caras
East Hampton, N.Y.

FOREWORD

When the sun goes down, the wild world does not go to sleep. The night shift takes over. Hawks are replaced by owls; chipmunks go to bed while mice venture forth; butterflies fold their wings under protecting leaves while long-tongued moths visit the flowers.

To know the night world we must use our ears. All of the nocturnal birds are quite vocal at times. The owls have distinctive voices; so have the whip poor-wills, nighthawks and others of their tribe. The woodcock on warm spring nights puts on a remarkable aerial display, but except for a few minutes in the deepening dusk we are denied a glimpse of the performer.

No doubt there is survival value in being nocturnal. Timorous beasties can more easily elude their pursuers in the dark, but they only partially succeed. Many predators have also evolved a nocturnal life style, using their keen sense of smell, acute hearing and heightened night vision to outwit their quarry.

On the other hand, for many desert animals, snakes especially, being nocturnal is necessary to survival because of the desiccating effect of the sun. The desert, deserted at mid-day, comes alive after sundown.

Go out some summer evening; walk a mile or two along an un-travelled rural road through the fields and woods and listen intently to the night sounds; not only to the obvious calls of owls (if you are lucky enough to hear them) but also to the piping and grunting of frogs and to the stridulations and trilling of crickets. See how many singers you can distinguish. The voices of the night are the voices of a world alien to most of us.

Roger Tory Peterson
Old Lyme, Connecticut

4

The pangolins (there are four species in Africa and three in Asia) are inoffensive, deliberate, but slow-moving creatures of the night. Some are arboreal, some burrow, but all seek a quiet life eating ants and termites by the pound. Since they are non-competitive and relatively helpless, night life suits them well—a time when they can be least visible and their privacy can have the best guarantee. They are so private and so nocturnal that people think they are rare even when they are not.

Pangolin

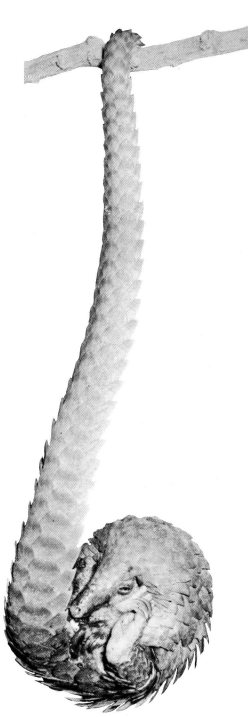

Slow Loris

For human beings the night signals danger more often than
it does security. Darkness holds what are apparently universal
dreads and so legends and stories have evolved to enable us
to handle our fears. Take the slow loris, among the least
offensive creatures in the world. Yet, wherever they are found
in Asia there are stories about their powers of evil. Some
people are absolutely terrified of them and liken them to witches
and demons. When you come upon them in the jungle at
night about all you see are two very large, very red eyes staring
back at your flashlight. Demons indeed!

Douroucou

Of all the monkeys only the douroucouli is
nocturnal. All other monkeys retire at dusk and
remain quietly hidden during the potentially
dangerous hours of the night. But, from
Nicaragua south to northeastern Argentina,
and from the Guianas and northern Brazil to
Peru and Ecuador, this small monkey with his
vocabulary of perhaps fifty different sounds
moves, feeds, mates and thrives at night. His
huge vocabulary helps his family group stay
in contact in the heavy foliage and the dark
hours. His eyes, of course, are outsized and his
night vision excellent. Competition pushed the
douroucouli past dusk into the night; his
adaptability enabled him to survive there.

Bobcat

It is not quite accurate to call the bobcat a night animal. Like many predators he is an anytime creature. Typically, the bobcat would cover his hunting circuit after dark if people and their dreaded dogs were near. In a remote area, one undisturbed or at least relatively so, the bobcat might hunt in broad daylight. It can be summed up this way: near man the bobcat's diurnal/nocturnal patterns are dictated by avoidance of danger. Away from man the same cat will simply follow his stomach.

Jaguarundi

The jaguarundi moves around by day and night,
sleeping when it feels like it, hunting when
hungry. It isn't as well adapted to life after dark
as the strictly nocturnal animals, of course, but
is probably helped by a strange and little-
understood sense we call the *kinesthetic*.
That refers to, roughly, a conditioned set of
muscular movements. It is a combination of
memory (body memory) and reflexes. We don't
understand it all that well, but it probably
helps cats like the jaguarundi handle the night
as well as they do the day.

Leopard Cat

Many people believe that cats can
see in the pitch black. If we are
to take *pitch black* as meaning
no light, nonsense. Cats can't see
when light is *absent* any better
than you or I can. What they can do
is see when there is little light.
Their eyes are enlarged and more
richly endowed with structures
called *rods* than ours are. That
enables them to make efficient
use of what little light there is at
night. It is believed by many that
they hunt and avoid danger by
sound as well. Their sense of
hearing is often amazingly keen.
All told, cats are beautifully adapted
to life after dark.

Timber Wolf

People, romantics that they are, usually regard
the wolf as a creature of the darkest most
dangerous hours. Since there is far more nonsense
than sense in print about the wolf, that isn't
surprising. Given a choice the wolf would
probably almost always be diurnal. His nocturnal
habits have been forced upon him by man.
In cases when the winter is severe and the wolf
is facing starvation he will hunt around the
clock, man or no man. But, we should think of
the wolf as an adaptable opportunist rather
than a night creature.

The springhare, just to put matters right, is a rodent, not a hare. (Hares and rabbits are lagomorphs, not rodents.) He is beautifully adapted to the night. He has a fine sense of smell, large and very sensitive eyes, and enormous ears that can catch the slightest sound. He needs all three for he is prey to many and is helpless except for his speed in getting away. But, that speed is useless unless you are warned in time. You can't run away once a cobra has struck or a leopard pounced. The springhare's existence depends on its ability to read the signals of the night.

Springhare

Spring Peeper

Rattlesnake

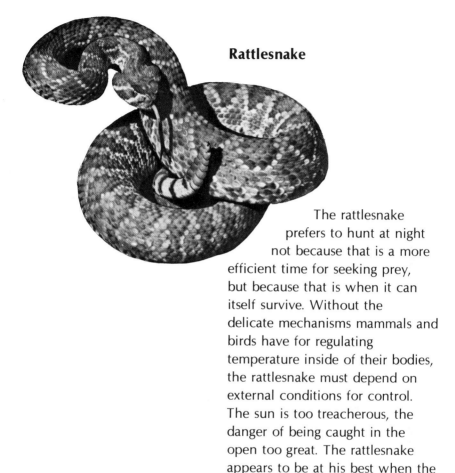

The rattlesnake prefers to hunt at night not because that is a more efficient time for seeking prey, but because that is when it can itself survive. Without the delicate mechanisms mammals and birds have for regulating temperature inside of their bodies, the rattlesnake must depend on external conditions for control. The sun is too treacherous, the danger of being caught in the open too great. The rattlesnake appears to be at his best when the temperature is between 72° and 82° Fahrenheit—night temperatures in many places where the rattlesnake survives.

Some sounds are so much a part of the night that our own reflexes have become conditioned to them. Blindfolded, anyone hearing the *peeping* of a spring peeper seeking his mate would not only know the season but the approximate place of the sun. The spring peeper is probably safer at night due to reduced predation and less desiccation by the sun's rays.

Green Turtle

The sea turtles provide us with a profound mystery.
How does an animal bobbing along at the surface
of the sea migrate over hundreds and hundreds of
miles to locate their natal beach, there to lay their
own eggs? We know they travel at night as well as
by day. Could it be that they use the sun and the
moon and the stars? They have to use something to
find their way across unmarked seas. Some people
are convinced the answer is celestial navigation.
It is an intriguing thought.

Colorado River Toad

If we want to understand the night world of a
frog or toad we must do away with our own
preconceptions of what the world looks like.
It is highly unlikely that a toad sees what we
see. He probably is acutely aware of movement,
something to be eaten or eaten by, but may
miss stationary objects altogether. It is hard
to look at the world through a toad's eyes,
but it makes more sense than looking through
our own and pretending we are seeing a toad's
world.

Green Tree Gecko

Given the number of things that like
to eat little lizards—birds, snakes,
mammals and not-so-little lizards—
being a little lizard would make
me very nervous. I would feel
somewhat better about it if I were
a green tree gecko operating my
bug-hunting business after dark.
Being roughly leaf-shaped, being
green, and being about when light
was low would make things easier,
at least emotionally. The combination
apparently works practically, too,
because there have been little
lizards running around after dark
for many, many millions of years.

Bandits always prefer the night, and raccoons are bandits. Whether it is a suburban garbage can or a woodland stream where crayfish and frogs abound the raccoon is always up to something somebody isn't going to like. The night suits this animal perfectly. He has good night vision, excellent hearing and lots of reasons for staying out of sight.

Raccoons

Striped Skunk

We think of a skunk's odor as a strictly defensive mechanism.
It is probably something more than that. It is probably a
means of communication in the dark hours when skunks
like to prowl. A light whiff discharged at will could help
prospective mates find each other, it could help young
follow their mother, and it could warn enemies away.
There is little doubt that at night the sense of smell takes on
added importance in the overall field of communications.

Peccaries, in a group, are able to stand off almost any enemy
that might make a pass at them. Because they often feed at
night when it is cool the members of a group have to have
a means of staying in contact with each other. Noise is the
answer. Peccaries are noisy eaters, noisy movers, noisy drinkers
and just plain noisy about everything. Their noises aren't
loud, or deafening or anything like that—but, more
importantly, they are constant. They are easy for other
peccaries to home in on.

Peccaries with Rattlesnake

Aardvarks

Large and pig-like, one of the world's most powerful burrowing
animals, the aardvark remains inoffensive. Like the other ant and
termite eaters (the pangolin, for example) it prefers to be left in
peace. Although occasionally abroad in daylight the aardvark is
usually curled away underground waiting for dusk. When she first
starts taking her baby on food-hunting forays the female never
moves around in daylight. Then, when she needs maximum security,
she moves only at night.

White-tailed deer

There are a number of reasons for an animal being active during the dark hours. For some it is the best time to find their prey, for others it is to avoid competition. For the deer, though, the night offers cover. A prey animal seeking no prey itself, it can survive best by moving about when least visible. Although sometimes active during the day and often quite busy at dawn and dusk, in areas where it senses danger the deer moves at night when it can feed in relative peace. Of course, there are predators at night as well. In each area the predators and the prey sort these things out among themselves and the whole system stays in balance until man stumbles into the middle of it.

Scops Owl

The owl's whole head is designed for
night reception. The eyes are extremely
sensitive to light. Because the owl is
notoriously far-sighted there are bristle-
like feathers around the base of its beak
for feeling the prey it has captured.
The dish-like shape of the face helps trap
and direct sound waves. An owl is like
some great integrated sensing device
in the night. Heaven help the mouse that
makes a move within that device's range
of detection.

When we look at an owl we see eyes, those enormous, obviously highly functional eyes. But, an owl listens. Sitting on a branch it waits for the incredibly small sound a mouse makes as it moves across the soft forest floor. Long before it can see the mouse the owl can locate it. Its hearing is much more directional than ours. It hears in three dimensions, while we hear in only two—on a horizontal plane. Without this special refinement the owl could not function at night.

Barred Owl

Just as the owl must be aware of every bit of sensory information available in order to hunt at night, it must offer as little information to its prey as possible if it is to succeed. An owl seeking prey is silent, it sits up above its prey's line of vision, and when it drops off its perch to soar down for the kill it is silent. Its feathers are constructed so that there is no noise, no rustle, nothing to warn an animal that talons are about to clamp it in a final vise.

Snowy Owl

Screech Owl

Fruit Bat

Unlike the insect-eating bats the flying foxes
or fruit bats have not developed the power
of echolocation. (There is one exception.)
Still, they are creatures of the night. They
have very light-sensitive eyes that help them
at dawn and dusk, but when it is really dark
they are quite helpless. They have to feel
their way around and locate the fruit they eat
by touch and smell. It is not the way we
think of bats at all.

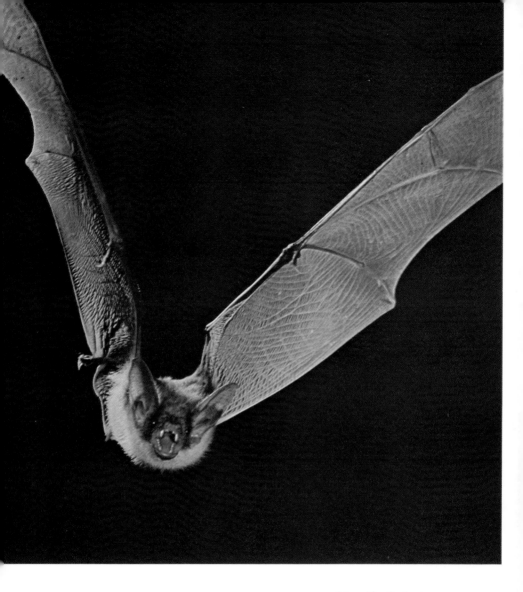

Myotis Bat

The insect-eating bats of North America see with their ears. They are sometimes referred to as *frequency-modulation* bats because of their almost unbelievable ability to vary a cry by a full octave in as little as one five-hundredth of a second. They are the originators of active sonar and locate both prey and obstacles with a stream of shrill cries well beyond the human range of hearing.

Ground Shark

There is an old wive's tale that sharks only attack prey
during daylight hours. That came into being because
it is during daylight when people are at the shore or
in the water. Sharks hunt when they are hungry—day
or night. In fact, those sharks that do attack man are
even more dangerous after dark because they are almost
impossible to see. It would be a sad mistake to depend
on a shark to retire at night.

Pacific Lobster

For crustaceans living in deeper parts of the sea
night and day are words without meaning. In shallow
water, however, there is a difference and it is at
night that lobsters are apt to be busiest digging
holes in the sea-floor or emerging from their hiding
places to crawl cautiously across open areas in search
of dead or living prey.

Tarsier

These tiny little primates have as their most conspicuous feature their enormous eyes, which isn't surprising for an animal that is so totally nocturnal. A tarsier, no more than three and a half to four inches long (discounting tail), will have eyes 5/8ths of an inch in diameter. In the same proportions a man six feet tall would have eyes almost thirteen inches across. That would make the face very untidy in a man, but on a tarsier that proportion looks both nice and natural.

The diminutive dwarf lemurs roll up in individual nests in the treetops or hide away in holes in their trunks. After dark, when the world is more to their liking, they emerge to seek their food and each other. Vocalization is somehow important to them and as the sun goes down they call across to each other like tenement ladies on their fire escapes. After dark has settled over the forest they come out, encounter each other like squirrels in their scampering movements and continue the conversations they started at long distance.

Dwarf Lemur

The small insect- and fruit-eating bat-eared fox of Africa is another of those creatures adaptable enough to live by night as well as by day. These little foxes often live near human habitations, apparently by choice, and will operate by day if unmolested. Let someone get a noisy or aggressive dog and the foxes locally will switch to night. One assumes their very large ears help them avoid trouble after dark and no one seems to know just how good their night vision may be.

Bat-eared Fox

Jaguar

Like any of the great cats the jaguar hunts
when it is safest to hunt. In remote areas,
seeking a deer or a tapir, there is no doubt
that a hungry *tiger* will seek prey by daylight—
probably not at high noon, but at least while
the sun is up. Let men with dogs move into
the area or let the jaguar get a taste for
livestock and night hunting will become the
rule. For some animals daylight is an essential,
for others the cover of darkness is the
ingredient that spells survival. For the
powerful spotted cat of the Americas either
will do—according to the dictates of
convenience.

Fennec

The fennec is the smallest of all the foxes. It has
the enormous ears so important to many night
creatures and it has night eyes, too. Light passing
through the retina has a chance to be absorbed.
If it is faint and isn't taken up it hits a mirror in the
fennec's eye and passes through the retina a second
time. That is an increase in efficiency over man
in dim light of 100%. It is just another of those
small adjustments nature makes for her creatures
and their survival opportunities. If we could
accomplish any one of them on our own it would
be called a miracle. Imagine that, a mirror in
each eye!

Oilbirds

The oilbird is one of two species that we know
for certain use echolocation in their nighttime
maneuvers. Asleep in caves during the day they
emerge at night to seek palm fruit whose oil content
gives them their name. They avoid collisions in
their permanently dark caves and amid the palms
by clicking at about 7000 sounds per second.
By judging the echos they can hear their way while
flying at considerable speeds. The only other bird
we are sure has this ability is the cave swiftlet
Callocalia.

I don't know why it is, but nocturnal creatures
seem to wear a look of permanent surprise.
The logical way to explain it is to refer to their
eyes, their great big eyes. But, there is more
to it than that. It is their whole expression,
their attitude. Perhaps it is that after living
at night for several hundred thousand generations
or more a species expects to be a secret. They
are surprised to learn that they are not and that
you know about them. Night animals do have
a special look.

Bushbabies

Potto

The potto's aversion to daylight is almost pitiful when
put to the test. It is not certain whether sunlight is
painful to them, but they act as if it is. During the day
they curl up in a hole or crevice in a tree and wait for
that awful sun to go down. They are completely adapted
to life at night. It suits their needs perfectly. They
probably feel very insecure when forced to expose
themselves to scrutiny in anything but the weakest
light—or red light—for perhaps like all night creatures
they are blind to red.

Tree Frog

There are sounds at night that can be startling. A tree frog when seized by a snake or raccoon can let loose a high-pitched scream that sounds very unfrog-like and the unwary human standing nearby may find his hair tending to rise. Actually, of course, the frog's distress is likely to be the more lasting.

Whipoorwill

For the man or woman afoot in the night there are sights that can give one pause. More than one after-dark stroller has found himself transfixed by a pair of ghostly, gleaming white eyes. It is nothing more than a whipoorwill waiting for an insect to happen by that suits its taste. Still . . . eyes in the night . . . .

Luna Moth

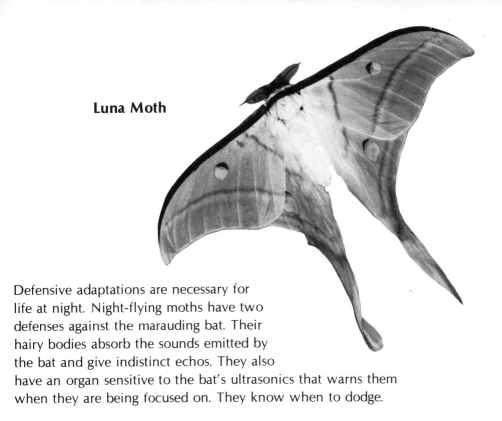

Defensive adaptations are necessary for
life at night. Night-flying moths have two
defenses against the marauding bat. Their
hairy bodies absorb the sounds emitted by
the bat and give indistinct echos. They also
have an organ sensitive to the bat's ultrasonics that warns them
when they are being focused on. They know when to dodge.

Katydid

The raucous katydids are strange creatures. The male alone
can *sing* (actually the *katydid* call is caused by a vibrating
membrane at the base of the right front wing), but if he hears
your approach he will stop. Probably a defense against predation.
They are very much a part of the summer night in the Eastern
part of North America.

Firefly

Fireflies aren't flies, they are soft-skinned beetles. It was once
thought that their light was produced by some kind of luminescent
bacteria. Such is not the case. They produce the light themselves
by converting nutrients into radiant energy instead of heat.
Their light has a short wavelength. It is apparently used
optionally. They usually opt for it when the sun is down since
it brings male and female fireflies together.

False Vampire Bat

There are false vampire bats in both the Old and the
New World. They are all characterized by their
absolutely enormous ears, designed by nature as
receivers for their endless squeaks and squeals at
extremely high frequencies. That erect device in the
ear is called a *tragus* and it apparently has some
special sensory function. We don't know very much
about it.

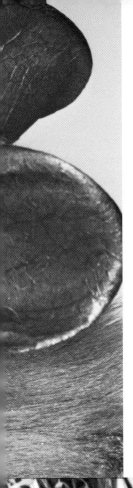

If the kangaroo rat were a daytime animal it could not live in the desert. The only way it can lose heat against a thermal gradient (where the air is warmer than it is) is through evaporative cooling. In order to stand the desert sun a kangaroo rat would have to lose through evaporation *every hour* water equivalent to 13% of its body weight. Obviously, for a kangaroo rat it is life at night or no life at all.

Kangaroo Rat

The world is hostile to the gray
fox. It is to all small predators.
He must hunt to live. He has no
choice in the matter. And so he
himself is hunted not only by
larger predators who have a
legitimate need of his flesh, but
by man and his agents. The fact
that man's animosity is misdirected
and even irrational doesn't help
the fox very much. So he often
hunts at night. He can find his
ground-nesting birds, then, his
frogs and toads and his occasional
barnyard fowl. The night is kinder
for a small, shy animal although
even the dark cannot protect him
from traps and poison. Being
a fox isn't easy, even if it is pretty.

Gray Fox

Coyote

Ring-tailed Cat

The ring-tailed cat is not a cat. It is one of the
Procyonidae and like its cousins the raccoon, the
coatimundi and the kinkajou it is nocturnal. It
negotiates cliffs and ledges at high speed in the
dark so those large eyes are not a luxury. It is also
apparently very sensitive to touch. Those long
whiskers and big ears also help open up the night.

The coyote is apparently capable of making any
adjustment necessary to avoid destruction. One of
them, predictably, is life at night. They function
perfectly well in daylight, but they like being where
and when man isn't. Who can blame them?

Vulpine Phalanger

When the marsupials spread out to
fill all the niches in the Australian
environments some, of course, had
to become nocturnal. The brush-
tailed opossums or vulpine phalangers
chose that route to survival. They
have learned to live in suburbs and
even cities, the only marsupials in
all of Australia that have learned
to capitalize on man—they often find
shelter in the roofs of his houses.
They are commonly found in gardens
and parks.

Octopus

The octopus is the highest of
the molluscs. Yet it has strangely
unintegrated senses. An octopus
is inspired to go after prey by
what it sees, but inspired to hold
it and eat it by what it tastes and
feels. If it feels a prey animal
but does not see it, its hunting
mechanism probably won't get
triggered. If it can see it but not
sense it with the suction cups
on its arms, it will be stymied.
The octopus has very large eyes
and it all seems to work out fine
in its twilight world amid the
bottom rubble.

Kinkajou

The kinkajou is not only nocturnal but almost entirely arboreal. It likes being off the ground and in the dark and with good reason. There are a lot of predators in the forests of southern Mexico, Central and South America. This little fruit-eater is better off out-of-sight. Strangely, though, they are noisy at night as they feed on fruit and insects. Their quavering scream is very shrill and can be heard for some distance. Why go to all the trouble of being nocturnal if you're going to be noisy?

Flying Squirrel

It is hard to imagine a creature less able to defend himself that a flying squirrel. Escape is about all he has going for him. While it is true that the night offers a blanket under which he can hide, it isn't altogether a secure world even then. Predators have adapted to the night just as their prey have. The flying squirrel must be as concerned about the owl as his diurnal cousins must be about the hawk. The world of night is as complete a system as the world of the sunlit hours.

Virginia Opossum

The opossum is at a disadvantage. It is a marsupial and in North America that hasn't been such a good evolutionary idea. It works well in Australia (at least it did until man got there) but here the placental mammals are far swifter in thought process and body movement. For the opossum the night represents a retreat to a time when competition and predation will be lowest. Bungling along through life as he does the opossum is better off at night. Of course, it has had at least one big disadvantage. The slow witted opossum has never been able to learn about cars. It just stands there staring into the headlights until it is too late—but, then, Mother Nature didn't have the automobile in mind when she helped the opossum evolve into a creature of the night.

PHOTO CREDITS